# Laughing Matters

A collection of humorous poems

Cathy Lawday

THE CHOIR PRESS

First published in the United Kingdom in 2026 by
The Choir Press

ISBN 978-1-78963-589-8

# ACKNOWLEDGEMENTS

Thank you to all the people who read or heard my poems and encouraged me to publish them, in particular readers of *Steeple Aston Life* magazine, members of Finstock and other Oxfordshire folkclubs, many supportive friends ... and Richard.

# CONTENTS

# Old Wife's Tale

*A friend's comment that there might be a body buried
under our patio  inspired me to write my first poem.*

I lie under the patio
Since my husband did me in
It's cold and dark and lonely
And I'm getting very thin.

It's pretty boring down here
It's dirty and it's damp
There's an awful lot of spiders
And I'd appreciate a lamp.

I miss the changing seasons
Down here it's dark and black
And it's particularly painful
Where he stabbed me in the back.

My only consolation
(And a constant source of cheer)
Is his new wife and her lover
And the schemes I overhear.

They whisper to each other
And what they plan to do
Is to murder the old bugger
So he'll end up down here too!

I'm absolutely overjoyed
I say with total candour
The sauce he served to me, his 'goose'
Will be perfect for the gander.

# The Patient Patient

*Due to Parkinson's Disease, I fall over fairly frequently.*
*This is the story of one trip to A & E.*

Last Saturday, I fell over. I swear I wasn't drunk
I just tripped over my own feet and went down with a thump.

My knees were first to hit the ground, and thereafter my chest
I was in shock for several minutes so I sat and had a rest.

I then assessed the damage. It was clear I was alive
And though I would be black and blue, I'd probably survive.

But as the afternoon wore on pain in my knee got worse
So I dialled 111 and was put through to a nurse.

She asked me all the questions that were required of her
Though I must admit I couldn't see how relevant they were.

She said, "I'll get a doctor to give you a call
Someone will ring within the hour. Tell them about your fall."

A doctor duly rang me after an hour at most
He said "You must see a doctor. Go to Bicester First Aid post."

So off we drove to Bicester where I retold my tale of woe
A nurse said "You need an X-ray. To Banbury you must go."

But first she took an hour or more to write out copious notes
And I took them with me, tucked into the pocket of my coat.

So back to Banbury we came, to the Horton A & E
Where a triage nurse asked me how I'd hurt my knee.

I told my story once again to this triage nursing sister
Who wrote down all I said and ignored the notes from
  Bicester.

After a ninety-minute wait I saw a very young MD
Who asked me what had happened and how I'd hurt my knee.

I then waited in a different place till by X-ray I was seen
And told my story to another nurse (who looked about 15).

I waited a while longer and had a little snooze
Till the young doctor came back and told me the good news.

He was very pleased to tell me it wasn't a disaster
I had not broken any bones. There was no need of plaster.

It'd be painful for a while and the bruises would be stunning
I'd need to take painkillers but I'd soon be 'up and running'.

But I felt that I had let them down, our hard-working NHS
I'd told my sorry story to six different folk, no less.

But what a boring tale it was: "I just tripped up and fell."
Couldn't I have come up with a more exciting tale to tell?

"I was abseiling down a tower. I was swimming with a shark"
"I was hunting with Bear Grylls in the Kruger National Park".

"I fell out of a window fleeing a jealous lover"
"I was doing a drugs deal when someone blew my cover".

I feel I have a duty to give the NHS a lift
To have a fascinating story to add excitement to their shift.

And I admit that I got bored telling every medic in the town
That I tripped over my own feet and just fell down.

# Christmas Spirit

Christmas comes but once a year
Perhaps that's just as well
Don't believe that stuff about good will
Christmas can be hell.

First there's the present-buying
Searching in every store
Trying to find a gift
For my bloody mother-in-law.

The shops are full to bursting
The assistants are all stressed
In the grotto, Santa's sweating
Bearded, booted, warmly dressed.

I've found gifts for everybody
Though spent twice as much as planned
I've even bought for my nephew
(The one that I can't stand).

I struggle through the crowded streets
Hear the Salvation Army singing hymns
Arriving home, I pretend it's summer
And have a glass of *Pimm's*.

My youngest son needs a costume
To play 'Shepherd Number 2'
It seems in these culturally sensitive times
A tea towel on the head won't do.

My daughter needs to take to school
Silver paper, card and glitter
I swear if I see the art teacher
I will struggle not to hit her.

The kids decorate the Christmas tree
Before they go to bed
On the top they put the angel
Who has somehow lost her head.

It's true the tree looks pretty
In silver, gold and scarlet
But it falls over in the night
And ruins the sitting room carpet.

On Christmas Eve I hang the stockings
Each dangling from its peg
Full of 'little fillers'
That cost an arm and leg.

Christmas Day begins for me
In the early hours of the morn
The turkey's so enormous
I have to start cooking it at dawn.

It's tricky getting the bloody bird
Into the roasting tin
So to give myself a boost
I have a tiny swig of gin.

Soon everyone's awake
All being very jolly
I take a nip from a bottle of rum
Hidden behind some holly.

Opening presents goes OK
With lots of fibs and flattery
But the kids are soon in a temper
Cos their new game has no battery.

I check up on the turkey
Which seems to be doing fine
And grateful for this miracle
I have a glass of wine.

At last it's time for Christmas lunch
I'm feeling rather merry
I don't care the turkey's over-cooked
Because I've been at the sherry.

Then we pull our crackers
What a waste of money
The toys inside are rubbish
And the jokes aren't even funny.

But everybody's festive
Their paper hats are on
I'm feeling almost mellow
… and the sherry's almost gone.

While they gather round the telly
And listen to the King
I feel the calm that only
A glass of port can bring.

We watch a silly film
The hero's a real twerp
I finish off the liqueur chocolates
And struggle not to burp.

By 5 o'clock the dog's been sick
The kids have begun to fight
The tree is leaning to the left
And I'm leaning to the right.

Then, thank God, it's teatime
Dad complains that the ham is tinned
Mum's got problems from eating sprouts
But luckily she's down-wind.

Getting the trifle from the fridge
I spot an opened bottle of wine
I take a swig of Chardonnay
And then I feel just fine.

The evening wears on slowly
Playing *Monopoly* and *Kerplunk*
At one point it occurs to me
That I might be slightly drunk.

Then the visitors put on their coats
They leave, and as they go
I head towards the washing up
And to a bottle of Bordeaux.

My husband thanks me for a lovely day
I say it was no trouble
I start to do some clearing up
Although by now I'm seeing double.

At last it's time for bed
I give a little festive cheer
And round off a successful day
With a can of lukewarm beer.

Christmas comes but once a year
Perhaps that's just as well
I usually survive the day
But the hangover is hell!

# An Intriguing Bit of Litter

*While taking part in a litter pick in my village I found a discarded
item which made me speculate on how it came to be there.*

There are many creatures
Who return every single year
To the place they always mate
Why they do it is not clear.

It is a basic instinct
Which they cannot fight
A strong primaeval feeling
Draws them to the site.

This is also true of humans
Some of whom return
Again and again to special places
After which they yearn.

It must've been this longing
Or something similar, I know not
Which caused an unknown woman
To park in a lonely beauty spot.

What her reasons may have been
I really can't suggest
But to this special place she came
And did a pregnancy test.

I found the test whilst volunteering
On the village litter pick
It was lying in the undergrowth
Almost hidden by a stick.

Weeks had passed before I found it
And so I do not know
If the result was positive or not
After time this did not show.

It seems the woman had not felt
The result would life enrich
Because she reacted to the test
By throwing it in the ditch.

Why did she come here to test?
I really cannot tell
I do not know her motives
(Perhaps it's just as well).

But my theory is that
The woman believed
This layby was exactly where
The baby could have been conceived.

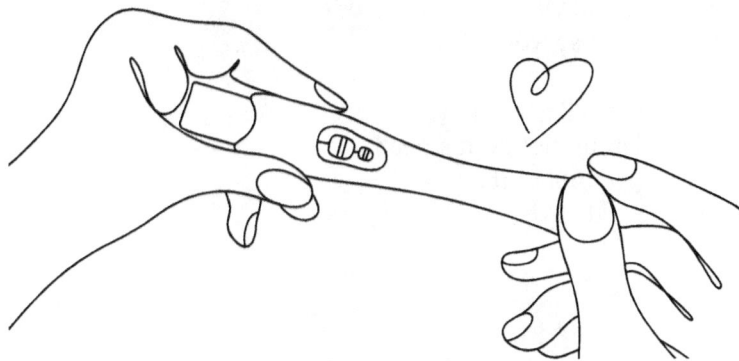

# Flexible Working

More and more folk are working from home
And giving their office a miss
And I'm guessing that lots of these people had thought
That working from home would be bliss.

No more commuter rush hour
No public transport pain
No bus or tube, no traffic queues
No hot and crowded train.

But there's a downside to flexible working
Your hours are not mainstream
You work any hour of the day or night
'Clocking off' is now just a dream.

The working day is dawn till dusk
But remember you're only a pawn
When the task in hand requires it
You work from dusk till dawn.

My editor rings at 5.58
Can I do revisions by 10.00 the next day?
"No problem. Of course I can do it"
Well, what else would I say?

I know that I'll get it done
I don't demur, not even a peep
After all, it's not as if
I really need to sleep.

Alone at home, you miss the office
The jokes, the birthday cakes
The chats by the coffee machine
And the memory of lunch breaks.

I've worked through holidays, Easter and Christmas
And there's no 'time off in lieu'
My husband complained about it
My children moaned at me too.

Oh, that familiar stab of guilt
Are my priorities right?
Let's have some quality family time now
(I can always work through the night).

So I'm not a flexible working fan
Because, between you and me
I can tell you from bitter experience
That the only flexible thing was me!

# Doing your Duty

When I got married to my husband
I found out far too late
That he had fixed ideas
And did not tolerate debate.

He said it was the duty
Of every married male
To teach his wife to cook and clean
And to do it without fail.

And furthermore it was the duty
Of every married chap
To help his wife remember this
By means of a little slap.

He kept a detailed record
Of things I couldn't do or couldn't cook
And made a note of all my crimes
In a little moleskin book.

My punishments he noted too
Neatly listing them all
Every punch and thump and kick
Every 'accidental' fall.

He made a note of every beating
Every hair-pull, every burn
He didn't like to do these things
But he said I had to learn.

He noted the occasion when
He knocked out my front teeth
Because I waved and said "Hello"
To our new neighbour, Keith.

He listed the week I spent in hospital
When he admits he "went too far"
After Keith gave me a lift to town
(Cos I wasn't allowed to use our car).

How I loathed that moleskin notebook
Which listed in such glory
All the awful details
Of my miserable story.

My husband is a big man
And a very powerful fella
So Keith and I had quite a job
To lock him in the cellar.

It's bare and damp and cold
In fact it's pretty bleak
But I only kept him down there
For a bit less than a week.

He always criticised my cooking
So I didn't give him any food
And at the end of a few days
He was really quite subdued.

I just needed those days
By hook or by crook
To see if I could find
The little moleskin book.

After a thorough search, I found it
And showed it to a nice PC
Who bagged it up as evidence
And said "Leave this to me."

The next time that I saw the book
It was an exhibit in the court
And for all my accusations
The book offered its support.

My lawyer said it was a duty
In which the jury must not fail
That men who beat their wives
Must spend some time in jail.

They retired to reach a verdict
Half an hour is all it took
Thanks to the corroboration
Of the little moleskin book.

When my ex-husband gets to jail
He may very soon discern
There are some prison practices
That he will have to learn!

But I do not care a jot
I won't hear him complain
Because Keith and I have moved
To a bungalow in Spain.

# Writing a Haiku

*A haiku is a Japanese 3-line poem. It has exactly 17 syllables which are arranged as 5 syllables in line 1; 7 syllables in line 2; and 5 syllables in line 3.*

| | |
|---|---|
| Sevn  teen  syll  a  bles | (5) |
| That's  not  much  space  to  com  ment | (7) |
| On  the  hu  man  race. | (5) |

| | |
|---|---|
| Sevn  teen  syll  a  bles | (5) |
| does  n't  give  much  time,  though  it | (7) |
| does  n't  have  to  rhyme. | (5) |

| | |
|---|---|
| Sevn  teen  syll  a  bles | (5) |
| A  short  span,  but  ev  ry  one | (7) |
| Does  it  in  Ja  pan. | (5) |

| | |
|---|---|
| At  temp  ting  to  write | (5) |
| A  hai  ku  is  a  tri  cky | (7) |
| Test  of  my  I  Q. | (5) |

| | |
|---|---|
| I  stru  ggle  to  write | (5) |
| A  form  I'm  not  sure  I  like | (7) |
| A  Ja  pa  nese  haik— | (5) |

# Old Soldier's Story

*After writing 'Old Wife's Tale' about a wronged wife buried under the patio, (see page 1) I remembered that previous occupants of our house found human remains whilst digging foundations for an extension. So here is another poem about a body under the patio.*

I lie under the patio
Cold and very dead
I'm resting on some concrete
And there's rubble round my head.

But I'm a total mystery
No one knows my name
I never featured on the News
Or came to *Crimewatch* fame.

I'm not the victim of a crime
I wasn't murdered by my wife
I didn't run up gambling debts
Or live a double life.

My death was pretty quiet
I just laid down to die
And all the other soldiers
Continued marching by.

As I lay in the coarse grass
Of this wholly foreign place
I thought about my family
And pictured my wife's face.

I smelled the sun-warmed earth
And realised, with a sigh
I'd never see my home again
Here was where I'd die.

And hundreds of years later
Excavating through the rock
The people living in this place
Will get something of a shock.

They'll inspect my ancient bones
And they'll try and guess
Who this age-old man can be
Among the building mess.

And eventually they'll understand
That once this man was me
A Roman soldier, who passed here
In about 44AD.

# Brain Surgery

In 2015, following medical advice
I had brain surgery to implant a device

A deep brain stimulator, which works
To reduce the twitches and the jerks

And the tendency to freeze
All the fun of Parkinson's Disease

During the procedure I was awake
Though sedated so I would not shake

And so every time there was a lull
In the sound of drilling in my skull

Light conversation I'd maintain
With a man whose hands were in my brain

What we discussed I have forgot
But I was awake and in earshot

And overheard things that were said
By the surgeon probing in my head

"Pass the tunnelling tool, please"
Was one which caused me some unease

Likewise, "Shall we stitch or glue?"
Which made me glad I had no view
Of what my brain was going through

He asked a nurse for suction
"To clear the debris out"

I said "Debris? Do you mind?
That's my brain you're talking about"

He said, "No, it's sawdust from the drilling"
A comment I found rather chilling

The surgeon's task was quite precise
To find a spot the size of a grain of rice

Once, while the op was underway
"Baby hippopotamus" I was asked to say

And asked to move my fingers to and fro
So the surgical team would know

They had found the perfect site
Not too far left, nor too far right

When they were satisfied with this test
The wire then travelled off south-west
Connected to the device implanted in my chest
(Which is not noticeable when I'm dressed)

At the time, the experience was surreal
But in retrospect doesn't seem that big a deal

I thought I'd become a figure iconic
But friends just joke and say that I'm bionic

I recharge the battery every ten days or so
Then I'm fully powered and off I go

It's true that Parkinson's isn't that funny
But the device keeps me going ... like a *Duracell* bunny

# Frustration

I'm a woman of maturer years
Long-married, content with my station
But in one area of my life
I suffer a certain frustration.

I'm certainly not in the first flush
I'm certainly not in fashion
But even a woman 'of a certain age'
Needs a bit of passion.

My husband's a considerate man
Kind, gentle and polite
But nowadays the thought of sex
Does not fill him with delight.

I don't want anything kinky
No *Fifty Shades of Grey*
Just a little bit more often
Than once a year on Christmas Day.

Last night I sprawled across the bed
With a sexy, silky teddy on
He just looked embarrassed
And said "Come on, girl. Steady on!"

I bought a little book
Of sex games and suggestions
But he took one look at the pictures
And said it was out of the question.

He won't try new positions
He says he's far too stiff
And I can only roll my eyes
And say to myself, "As if ..."

My husband's a considerate man
Polite and gentle and kind
But these days when it comes to sex
He is truly disinclined.

Sometimes, watching TV, he shouts "Yes!"
And I think that I'm in luck
But the only tackle that interests him
Is in the England ruck.

I've abandoned being subtle
Now I give a clear indicator
I lay out batteries on the bed
Next to the vibrator.

I've tried all kinds of lingerie
Even crotchless knickers
But on his erotic meter
The needle barely flickers.

I wore a French maid's outfit once
With an apron, lacy and frilly
My husband took one look and said
"Now you're just being silly."

I bought an intriguing sex toy
A sort of vibrating clamp
But he refuses to try it
He says it'll give him cramp.

We needn't worry about contraception
Now I'm over the hill
We can frolic unrestrained
By coil, cap, sheath or pill.

But such freedom is wasted
On a man in the autumn of his life
Who seems to have forgotten
How to fancy his wife.

My husband's a considerate man
Gentle, polite and kind
But he's lost all his enthusiasm
For doing the bump and grind.

When we first got married
He was always 'in the mood'
But since he reached retirement age
He's become something of a prude.

This red-blooded man of mine
Once couldn't get enough
But now that he's of golfing age
He's just run out of puff.

He took up other interests
And as the years advance
He seems totally indifferent
To doing the mattress dance.

I know I'm no spring chicken
And time has left its mark
But we can pretend to be young again
When we're in the dark.

Once the light is off
We can get down and dirty
And then it's easy to forget
We're nearer seventy than thirty.

My husband's a considerate man
He's kind and he's polite
But I wish he had more interest
In the antics of the night.

My husband is a lovely man
He is kind and he is gentle
But once in a while when it comes to sex
I wish he'd just go mental!

# The Remains of Empire

We're having a Platinum Jubilee
There are revels all over the nation
To celebrate a record reign
Of seventy years duration.

There are parties, picnics and pageants
Processions, and all kinds of bash
And many manufacturers
Have seen a chance to make some cash.

There are jubilee plates on sale
Jubilee tea towels, jubilee jugs
Jubilee pens and pencils
Jubilee beer glasses, jubilee mugs.

There are games too – Jubilee Bingo
and Pin the Jewel on the Crown
Packs of jubilee playing cards
And a jubilee dressing  gown.

A jubilee cup and saucer and teaspoon
A key ring, an apron, a bell
A flower pot, a shopping bag
A jubilee teapot, and tea as well.

But the worst example of merchandise
That I have so far seen
 Is a little clockwork figure
Of a plastic dancing queen.

Companies are cashing in
Selling their jubilee merch
But to find items made in England
You really have to search.

Most of this stuff is made overseas
In India, China, Hong Kong
Is this what is left of the Empire
Its ultimate swan song?

I'm not a great fan of the monarchy
I can't say that I'm pro-royal
But to this frail old lady
I feel surprisingly loyal.

And so I hope that Her Majesty
Doesn't stop to think
That this souvenir tat is all that remains
Of the world map that once was all pink.

# The Joys of Spring

It's time to spring into action
Time to find
That springy things will
Spring to mind.

Spring into life
Spring forward not back
Spring to attention
Get on track.

Eat your spring greens
Spring onions, spring lamb
Spring a friend from prison
If you can.

You're no spring chicken
But even so
Put a spring in your step
And away you go.

Visit hot springs
They're good for your skin
Leap from a springboard
Jump right in.

Ignore spring cleaning
That's a bore
Spring's the time for a break
Not a chore.

Springtime is the time
To see Paris, France
Time to sing and
Time to dance.

On your spring mattress
Lose control
Release your spring fever
Have a spring roll.

# Zoom

The damned corona virus was the cause of doom and gloom
So to subvert its limitations we all signed up to *Zoom*.

Work meetings, webinars, quizzes, these could all resume
Family chats and book groups could all be done on *Zoom*.

The picture sometimes disappeared and then so did the sound
And a noise like running water could be heard in the
  background.

One soul didn't know how to mute or how to leave the room
But pretty soon we got the hang of how to meet on *Zoom*.

Many companies went bust but others had a boom
And I'm betting it was all good news for the people who own
  *Zoom*.

Future generations will use this system from the womb
And will think there's nothing strange about a life lived just
  on *Zoom*.

And older generations will use this method, I assume
To send us ghostly messages from far beyond the tomb.

# New Year, New Me

A new year, and a new leaf
Going to colour my hair and whiten my teeth
Going to get fit. Going to join a gym
Going to start that diet. Going to get slim.

Going to learn a foreign language and how to type
Going to keep in touch on *Zoom* and *Skype*
Going to read more books, watch less TV
Going to meditate. Going to 'just be'.

Going to eat more veg, use the exercise bike
Going to do my yoga and regularly hike
Going to be more forgiving, less judgmental
Going to stop thinking all MPs are mental.

Going to be nicer to my family, thoughtful and kind
If they annoy me, I won't mind
The only drawback I foresee
Is nobody will know it's me.

# A Lot of Hot Air

I've watched on television
Cookery programmes galore
Countless different chefs
Both part-time and hard-core.

Nadia, Nigella, Jamie
Rick Stein and all that fish
Ainsley, Gordon, Delia
Each with their 'signature dish'.

Chefs from India, China, Italy
All cooking with panache
They made it look so simple
I thought I'd have a bash.

I felt that anything was achievable
Even for me, a total beginner
So I decided to spread my wings
And cook my partner dinner.

I decided to make a soufflé
And serve it up with flair
It shouldn't be that difficult
After all, it's mostly air.

I started on the recipe
I had 8 eggs to separate
But the yolks just kept breaking
They would not co-operate.

My sister-in-law, who is a chef
Says confidence is what cooks need
So I confidently mixed the yolks and whites
And paid the recipe no heed.

I whisked them all together
I thought it would be fine
I bunged it in the oven
Then checked the quality of the wine.

I kept opening the oven door to check
But the soufflé just seemed to sink
It didn't rise as it should have done
So I had a little think.

Desperate, I turned to the internet
And asked if anyone out there
Could tell me why my soufflé
Wasn't full of air.

I got a variety of answers
One from a man who was quite good-looking
But I couldn't see how photos of his genitals
Would help me with my cooking.

I said farewell to my new pals online
And continued to struggle unaided
By now the novelty had worn off
And I was feeling rather jaded.

I laid my dinner table
With the best cutlery and glass
I found a couple of candles
Which added a bit of class.

When my beloved came home from work
I told him there was a surprise
I'd made a soufflé for supper
If only it would rise.

The bloody souffle wouldn't set
It looked like a bowl of slop
I tried turning up the oven
But that just burnt the top.

Eventually I brought it to the table
And served my love a portion
He tasted the lumpy liquid
With a certain amount of caution.

"I appreciate your effort"
He said, wiping egg off his lips
"But I think it would be a good idea
If I went and got fish and chips".

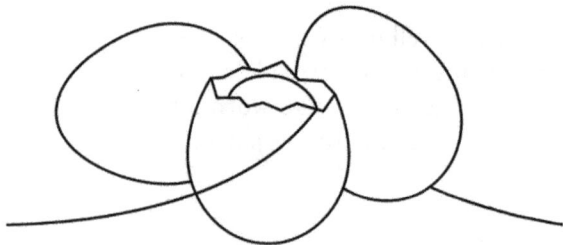

# Trading Up

There's hot news in the village
Tongues are wagging without cease
Bernard Miller's left his wife
And gone off with a flighty piece.

The gossips are in outrage
They're furious, they're mad
She's only in her thirties
He's old enough to be her dad!

It's an old and banal story
The way men see it as a doddle
To dump their wife of 30 years
And trade her in for a newer model.

He's treating his spouse just like a car
That he no longer needs
He wants a flashy racer now
Built not for comfort, but for speed.

It's such a heartless thing to do
Bernard obviously has no feeling
Just because her assets these days
Are nearer the carpet than the ceiling.

It's true that she has wrinkles
And lines upon her face
But she has lived with Bernard
So it's no surprise that is the case.

His wife has very mixed feelings
About the current parting
She certainly won't miss
His nightly snoring or his farting.

She views Bernard's departure
As an opportunity for her
To find somebody younger too
A 'new man', as it were.

She won't be satisfied with a bigot
Like Bernard, that's for sure
A boozing, belching sexist
An unreconstructed bore.

She's wasted too many years
Washing Bernard's socks and pants
Listening to his reactionary views
His unedifying rants.

She's certain that she doesn't want
Anyone like the man she wed
She's hoping for something different
Particularly in bed.

She's hoping to try out
The occasional new position
After all, she's old enough
Not to have to ask permission.

She's game for anything once
She longs for something new
She'd even try a threesome
(As long as it was somebody she knew).

So when Bernard's young lady
Finds life with him begin to pall
When she kicks him out and back
To his old lady he has to crawl.

He'll find she no longer wants him
After all, it's not just men
Who get tired of their old banger
Trade up, and start again.

# A Visit from the Grandchildren

When my grandchildren come to stay
The day starts at 5.30 on the dot
When the youngest one manages somehow
To climb out of the cot.

Her father slept in that cot contentedly
Till he was over three
But my granddaughter is more adventurous
And is determined to cut free.

She comes into our big bed
Which suddenly seems quite small
With a little person wriggling about
It's a brutal wake-up call.

She pokes her finger up my nose
And bounces on my chest
There is no hope of a quiet cuddle
Or a half hour more of rest.

By six all three of them are awake
Running around in pjs and bare feet
I consult the notes I have been given
About what they're allowed to eat.

All these suggestions are rejected
They don't want fruit, yoghurt or porage oats
After losing the negotiation
I cook them all french toast.

At eight o'clock there's a moment's peace
They're all inside a 'den'
Made of chairs and my best tablecloth
It's quiet for nearly 3 minutes, then . . .

The den collapses in a tangled heap
On the kitchen floor
And this is so hilarious
They do it three times more.

By 10 o'clock they're finally dressed
Though it took quite some persuasion
One has insisted his *Spiderman* costume
Is right for the occasion.

The other can't wear his clean t-shirt
Because "it's not a yellow day"
So he asks if he can wear the dirty one
And I say that's OK.

The little girl thinks her ballet skirt
Will be just right for a trip to the swings
It's an interesting outfit
Tutu, wellies and angel wings.

We set off for the park on foot
I'm pushing the buggy, a scooter and a bike
My grandson helpfully suggests
I can ride one if I like.

At the park, one wants pushing on the swing
Number 2 wants catching  at the end of the slide
Number 3 has fallen off the monkey bars
And has bruised his elbow and his pride.

Then it's off to the nearby café
And babyccinos for everyone
I ignore the list of approved foods
And buy each of them a large sticky bun.

On the walk home from the park
I thought they would be tired
But (possibly due to the sugary bun)
All three children seem to be wired.

Once we get home I plonk them all
In front of daytime telly
They are transfixed by the Kardashians
While I prepare beans on toast and jelly.

After lunch the little one
Goes down for her afternoon nap
I look at her sleeping form with envy
And suggest that the boys play *Snap*.

The rules are freely interpreted
It seems I cannot win
So I change the game to who can throw
Most cards into the wastepaper bin.

The afternoon winds slowly down
We decide to do some baking
Though so much raw mixture gets eaten
That it's hard to know what we're making.

They eat their home-made biscuits
And pack some to take home for tea
They'll be on a sugar high for hours
But that doesn't bother me.

At six their parents come to collect them
And I'm sorry to see them leave
My granddaughter gives me a teary cuddle
And leaves a trail of snot on my sleeve.

With hugs and kisses they say goodbye
Then into the kitchen I creep
I wrap myself in my best tablecloth
Crawl into the den, and fall asleep.

# Dick Pics

'Well-endowed of Witney' please don't send
More photos of your schlong
I'm really not that interested
In the dimensions of your dong.

I do not want to see
More close-ups of your chopper
Even though you have assured me
It is something of a whopper.

I've said before, I think dick pics
Are desperately silly
And I invariably snigger
At the photos of your willy.

I'm aware that this will sound
Particularly callous
But I simply shriek with laughter
At photos of your phallus.

You regularly tell me
That you've got wood
Well I'd use it for kindling
If only I could.

I've no desire wish to view the snaps
Of your member tumescent
Not even the occasion
When you painted it fluorescent.

Do not send another video
Of you giving it a jiggle
That just provoked
A hysterical giggle.

I am not turned on
By magazines on the top shelf
So keep your antics with the rubber doll
Strictly to yourself.

As for the photo with tinsel
You sent for the festive season
Please note that they're called 'private parts'
For a very good reason!

I fought to forget
Throughout all December
The memory of your bauble-bedecked
Private member.

I honestly do not want to see
Your sausage, your trouser peg
Your todger, your John Thomas
Your willy wonka, your wooden leg.

No matter what you call it
Pecker, peter, prick or sword
This avalanche of photos
Is making me s-o-o bored.

Put away your pink oboe
Your python, your tool
You want me to think you're sexy
But I just think that you're a fool.

It may be important to you
But to me it's a mere trifle
To get yet another snapshot
Of you polishing your rifle.

Your ego is fragile
And I'm sorry to dent it
But 'dick' refers <u>not</u> to the picture
But to the idiot who sent it.

Your member may be upstanding
But I am not impressed
So please put away your winkle
And  for heaven's sake ... **get dressed!**

# RHS Garden, Wisley

*This silly poem came about in reply to a challenge —*
*could I write a poem that rhymed with 'Wisley'?*

We're on the motorway
People driving busily
They're on their way to work
But we're going to Wisley.

At home the weather was cloudy
Mizzly and drizzly
But we had a sunny day
When we were at Wisley.

It's not that far away
We drove there quite easily
Just a 90-minute drive
To get to Wisley.

It was Flower Show week
Numbers increased visibly
Lots of extra visitors
Enjoying the sights of Wisley.

People unpacking their sandwiches
Opening their bottles of fizzly
Enjoying a picnic lunch
On the lawns at Wisley.

Then it's time to leave
Children are getting grizzly
Pack up your things and go
Say goodbye to Wisley.

# An Email from Irina

Today when I opened my emails
Among all the usual spam
Was a message from someone called Irina
Who clearly thought I was a man.

She seed me in the workplace
And felt I had some lovely eyes
And I also look more handsome
Than some other of those guys.

She has to go home to Bulgaria
Because her job has come to end
But she can stay in England longer
If I like and be her friend.

She had job in a nursing  home
And she loved the old folk in her care
But then the boss had give her sack
It really wasn't fair.

She gone outside for just a minute
To make a very quick smoke
She and Jan the maintenance man
Had been doing a private joke.

They were gone into the woodshed
To keep out of the rain
She took off her underwear for dry
And was put it on again.

Jan had frostbite in his two hands
Because washing the boss's car
And so to thaw him fingers
He had them in her bra.

But the boss just didn't listen
She thinks he has prejudice about Bulgaria
He says he never again hire anyone
From 'that whole bloody area'.

But she got no home in Bulgaria
Cos her husband threw her out
He thinks she make hanky-panky
With an old and wealthy Kraut.

She was help the German tourist
Find his way around the town
His moneybelt get mix up in his clothing
So that why his lederhosen were down.

He give her 20 US dollars
For helping him find the way
But her husband don't believe it
And kick her out without delay.

Next she met a Dutchman
He was lovely chap
But he stop help her when his wife
See Irina sitting on his lap.

So now no job, no home. no husband
She just got very bad luck
But if I would help her stay here
She'd repay me ...

# Ageing is No Fun

Ageing is no fun
It creeps up on you without warning
And you finally realise you're old
One depressing morning.

Your skin is full of wrinkles
Your assets are heading south
There's the hint of an incipient
Moustache around your mouth.

You've got less hair than you used to have
It gets sparser every day
And what hair you have left
Is predominantly grey.

You can't get out of a low chair
Without an unseemly grunt
And you got dressed without your glasses
So your sweater's back to front.

People offer you their seat
When you  travel on the train
Which is very kind of them
But is depressing just the same.

Someone behind you in the checkout queue
Sighs loudly when you drop your purse
And then the assistant says "Bless"
Which is very much worse.

You keep your mobile phone in your handbag
With your bus pass, keys, your pills, some tissues, a comb,
a shopping list, two out-of-date money-off coupons, your
glasses, a dried-up bottle of scent, a nail file, 2 random
buttons, an ancient lipstick, a bulldog clip and other useful
   things
Which means that you can't find it
If ever it rings.

And when your body lets you down
With surprise attacks of gas
There's nothing you can do
Except wait for it to pass.

But worse than all of these indignities
Oh alas, alack
Is when you look into the mirror
And see your mother looking back.

# Chocoholic

There is no doubt about it
If I had to choose
To save my grandson or a bar of chocolate
The child would surely lose.

It's not that I don't love him
He is a lovely little boy
But he doesn't give me what chocolate does
That sheer, unbridled joy.

That luxurious, velvety texture
As it melts upon the tongue
There simply is no other food
From which such pleasure can be wrung.

I know that chocolate isn't healthy
It doesn't do you good
But that just adds to its attraction
Knowing it's a 'naughty' food.

Though cocoa beans are a vegetable
And must count as one of your five-a-day
And if you have *Fruit and Nut*
You're not going far astray.

It is said of middle-aged English women
That they like gardening more than sex
Well, I think chocolate's even better than both
(Or it was last time I checked).

So let's hear a cheer for chocolate
That provider of positive feeling
It should be available on the NHS
For its infallible powers of healing.

When chocolate finally kills me
As it eventually will
I will leave this world with no regrets
I'll know I had my chocolate fill.

When you plan my funeral
Include in your accounting
The cost of providing at my wake
An enormous chocolate fountain.

If I go to heaven
I'll meet St Peter at the gate
And I hope he'll welcome me to paradise
With a box of *After Eight*.

And if I wind up in the other place
Well, that has advantages too
The flames of hell will work a treat
On my chocolate fondue.

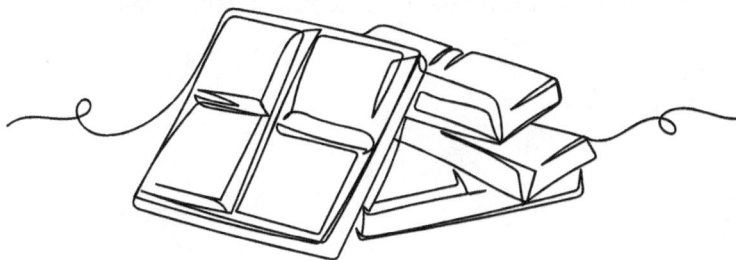

# Escaping the Present

We're seeking some frivolity, some silliness, some froth
As an antidote to the modern world and all its rage and wrath
Let us leave the present, spend an hour in a costume drama
To escape depressing documentaries, *Newsnight*, *Panorama*.

When a lady's main concern was having a waist of 18 inches
Achieved by firmly lacing up the whalebone till it pinches
In the boudoir a maid helps madame put on her bustle
Downstairs the doorbell rings and the butler starts to buttle.

Never mind the heroine can't breathe inside that brutal corset
She's got an invitation to dine with Lady Dorset
Who cares that she'll be poisoned by the arsenic in her wig
She's hoping that Lord Bridgerton will ask her for a jig.

Tales of romance and intrigue among the landed gentry
Where those of independent means lived a life of plenty
Where dressers, maids and valets knew all there was to know
About affairs above the stairs and also those below.

Where women would retire and leave men to pass the port
To discuss matters of importance or what's happening at court
Where the wealthy have a box at the opera or the ballet
And complain how difficult it is to find a decent valet.

Where staircases and titles and houses are all grand
And heroes own a country pile with many acres of land
Where bodices are ripped and proposals are indecent
Where we can happily forget anything more recent.

Give us *Downton*, give us *Bridgerton*, give us *The Gilded Age*
Where cotillions and waltzes dance right off the page
Give us boudoirs, powder rooms, bedchambers and bordellos
Give us another story from the pen of Julian Fellowes
Let's leave depressing documentaries, *Newsnight*, *Panorama*
And while away an hour in the world of a costume drama.

# Fit for Publication

*This poem was written in response to a complaint from the designer of*
*the village magazine that my poems were too long to fit on the page.*

It seems I am the cause of editorial unease
To fit my poems on the page is something of a squeeze.

The poor designers reduce the size of the type
Shrink the space between verses and try not to gripe.

And though not wishing to be seen as a prude
The editor removes a verse  he thinks is too rude.

So this time I'm going to try and be brief
Cos my verbosity is really the cause of some grief.

My poems tend to be rather loquacious
And the publication isn't sufficiently spacious.

So I trust I don't leave you feeling a bit miffed
That you've had short measure, or even short shrift.

I hope this  poem's truncated extent
Does not lead to feelings of real discontent.

The motive for this work's succinct duration
Is to preclude the editor's frustration.

For once I'm doing what I oughta
And so this poem is decidedly shorter.

# Rain On Our Parade

*A heartfelt plea to the weather gods on the eve of*
*King Charles' coronation.*

Rain, rain go away
Come again another day
People would be so dismayed
If it rained on our parade
For the coronation of the King
So please don't dampen everything.

I know you make the rivers flow
And give succour to all things that grow
But please could you just stay away
I only ask it for one day
Because you have it in your power
To ruin the day with a heavy shower.

And a full-on downpour really could
Change the soccer pitch into a field of mud
That would curtail the planned pursuits
Out would come macs and welly boots
Rain would soak through the summer frocks
And seep right into shoes and socks.

The glimpse of springtime so revered
Would suddenly have disappeared
And winter's back – cold, damp and wet
And summer would feel months off yet
Then suddenly there is a shout
Cheer up and smile! "The sun's come out"!

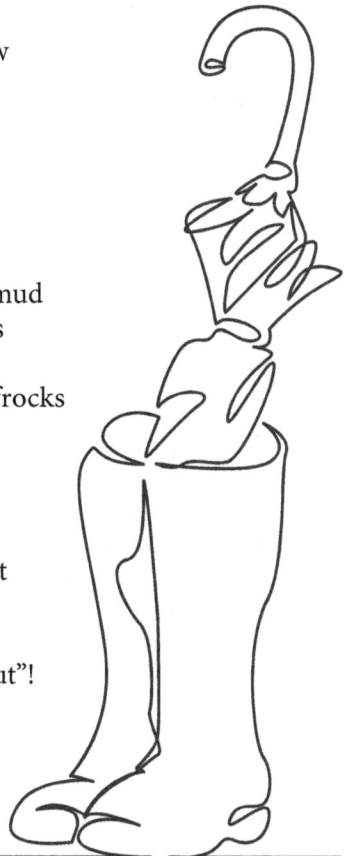

# You Have Been Warned!

I'm getting rather tired
Of being treated like a shmuck
With cautions, warnings and advice
Everywhere I look.

It's assumed I have no judgment
That I have no nous
And I will surely kill myself
In various ways about the house.

There's a warning on the bottle
That I must not drink the bleach
Should there also be a sticker
'Don't eat the stone' on every peach?

If I buy a dozen eggs
Should it say 'Don't eat the shell'?
Should it tell me 'Don't eat the wax'
On a mini *Baby Bel*?

'Not to be used as a hair dryer'
Says the label on a paint-stripping tool
I'm told that the kettle 'will generate heat'
Do they think I'm a total fool?

The label on a recent purchase
Really made me see red
I bought a little mirror
'Contains glass' the label said!

I have discovered for myself
That knives may lead to cuts
And I can work out on my own
That peanut butter contains nuts.

I know the picture on the packet
Is only a 'serving suggestion'
And that if I eat the packaging
It'll give me indigestion.

I'm aware things coming from the oven
Will probably be hot
And that things taken from the freezer
Will probably be not.

I know not to snack on poison ivy
Or attempt electrical repairs
To take a stroll in quicksand
Or wear roller blades on the stairs.

Do they think that we are stupid
With not an ounce of common sense?
Well if we really are that daft
Safety advice is no defence.

The independent among us
The risk-takers, the mindless
When faced with these alerts and alarms
Opt for a sort of blindness.

When we see a warning label
We choose not to heed it
We throw away the instruction book
Sure that we don't need it!

Enough with all these cautions!
Away with words of warning!
Being careful all the time
Is just so bloody boring!

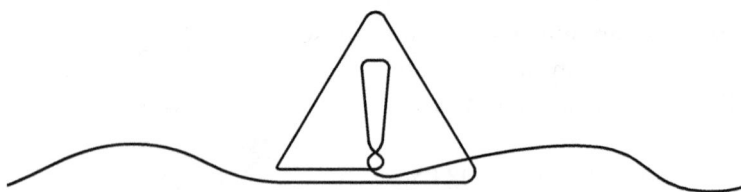

# I'm Not a 'Proper' Poet

I am under no illusion
I know I'm not a 'proper poet'
My son will kindly point it out
In case I didn't know it.

What I write is just doggerel
Dee dum, dee dum, dee dum
It has a simple rhythm
Which makes the mind go numb.

What's worse, it usually rhymes
Which proves that it is frivolous
Because poetry that rhymes
Is viewed as childish and ridiculous.

My poems are mildly amusing
Which makes them seem old-fashioned
Compared to modern rap
Which is angry and impassioned.

My poems aren't obscure
They leave no room for doubt
You don't have to read them several times
To decipher what they're about.

They have proper punctuation
No *e e cummings* nonsense
They also have capital letters
And full stops for every sentence.

My poetry is not baroque
Not flowery nor florid
There are no elaborate metaphors
Or descriptions verging on torrid.

My poetry is not ambiguous
It is not murky or opaque
Its meaning is quite obvious
(Provided you're awake).

So do not judge it harshly
I know it is not Keats or Shelley
It's just harmless entertainment
Like watching quizzes on the telly.

Do not be too critical
Don't be pretentious or worse
Don't get too high-falutin'
When judging my humble verse.

Cos if I'm not a proper poet
That makes my poetry improper too
And my next improper poem
Might be all about you!

www.ingramcontent.com/pod-product-compliance
Lightning Source LLC
LaVergne TN
LVHW041208080426
835508LV00008B/852